TAROT

FOR SELF-GUIDANCE
AND AWARENESS

SHELTER HARBOR PRESS

NEW YORK

JOHANNES FIEBIG & EVELIN BUERGER

TAROT

FOR SELF-GUIDANCE
AND AWARENESS

I

THE MAGICIAN

LIBRARY OF ORACLES

Tarot: Oracle, Advice, Self-Help

This edition published by Shelter Harbor Press by arrangement with Alexian Ltd.

Shelter Harbor Press
603 W. 115th Street
Suite 163
New York, NY 10025

For sales in North America and UK, please contact
info@shelterharborpress.com

Picture credits
All images included in this volume are in the public domain, with the exception of the following, for whom the publishers gratefully acknowledge permissions:

Cover design: Jessica Quistorff in use of the images from fotolia.com "fairy forest" © vsurkov and "beauty frame" © aalto
Images: Tarot de Marseille – Convos. By Otto Spalinger. © 1999 AGM AGM-Urania, www.tarotworld.com
Translated from the German language by Ulrich Magin
Book design: Jessica Quistorff and Antje Betken; ornaments by Hermann Betken in use of the image from fotolia.com "beauty frame" © aalto
Typesetting, artwork, image selection: Antje Betken

Original German Edition: © 2014 by Koenigsfurt-Urania Verlag GmbH

Cataloging-in-Publication Data has been applied for and may be obtained from the Library of Congress

ISBN: 978-1-62795-021-3

Printed and bound in China

10 9 8 7 6 5 4 3 2 1

ABOUT THE AUTHORS

Evelin Buerger, born in Kiel in 1952, and Johannes Fiebig, born in Cologne in 1953, live together near the city of Kiel, Germany.

They are among the world's most successful authors on the subject of Tarot; having sold more than 1.7 million of Tarot books worldwide.

In 1989, Bürger and Fiebig founded the publishing house Königsfurt Verlag, in Germany that has since merged to become Königsfurt-Urania.

CONTENTS

Welcome to the world of Tarot 10

Everyday Spreads.. 13

Alternative Spreads.. 14

The Major Arcana 15

    The Magician 16

    High Priestess 18

    Empress 20

    Emperor 22

    The Pope 24

    Lovers 26

    Chariot 28

    Justice 30

    Hermit 32

    Wheel of Fortune 34

    Strength 36

    Hanged Man 38

    Death.. 40

    Temperance 42

    Devil 44

    Tower 46

    Star 48

    Moon 50

    Sun 52

    Judgement 54

    World 56

    Fool 58

The Minor Arcana 61
The Wands.. 62
   Ace.. 62
   Two 63
   Three 64
   Four 65
   Five 66
   Six 68
   Seven 70
   Eight 71
   Nine 72
   Ten 74
   Page 76
   Knight 78
   Queen 80
   King 82

The Cups 84
   Ace.. 84
   Two 86
   Three 88
   Four 89
   Five 90
   Six 92
   Seven 93
   Eight 94
   Nine 96
   Ten 98
   Page 100
   Knight 102
   Queen 104
   King 106

The Swords 108
    Ace 108
    Two 109
    Three 110
    Four 112
    Five 114
    Six 115
    Seven 116
    Eight 118
    Nine 120
    Ten 122
    Page 124
    Knight 126
    Queen 128
    King 130

The Pentacles 132
    Ace 132
    Two 134
    Three 136
    Four 138
    Five 140
    Six 142
    Seven 144
    Eight 146
    Nine 148
    Ten 150
    Page 152
    Knight 154
    Queen 156
    King 158

Welcome to the world of Tarot

Would you like to experience more love and feel comfortable in your relationships? Do you desire happiness and greater success? Then you've come to the right place! Tarot is the smarter way: if at first you get stuck, build a bridge. The symbols on the cards show you new paths. Try them. Opportunities will then open up in real life.

Back to the roots ...

In this book, we deliberately use the old images of the *Tarot de Marseilles*. This helps to concentrate our minds and to evoke our own creative experiences during card reading. The beautiful images of the Rider Waite cards are great, but they can often feel so well-known that they seem no longer to inspire wonder, to produce no basic surprise when turning the cards.

For that, reading the cards with the *Tarot de Marseilles* is one of the approved remedies. It is good training for going back to the basics of interpretation.

Well – to take an example, the cups represent the element of water, and water refers to the soul and psyche, to feeling, desire, and faith. The cards with the no. 1 (the aces) concentrate the whole essence of the respective element; the cards with the no. 2 depict basic contradictions or complements of the respective element; and the cards with the no. 3 symbolize a first solution or a new problem, etc. So, two cups mean basic contradictions or complements of feelings, desires, or faith; three cups represent a first solution or a new problem for emotional issues, etc.

... create a new future

In this way, we gain creativity and pleasant surprises while card reading. The antique style of the Tarot de Marseilles (which was the second kind of Tarot – after the Visconti Tarot, created in the early 16th century) makes it easy to open the mind to personal ideas and impressions. These historic images supply open sources, unladen structures of interpretation. This opens you up to working with the significance of a card. Thus, you will find new personal meanings. These will prove to be the keys to new doors in your life.

The crucial point: Experience your personal magic

This book opens with *The Magician*: a wonderful card to experience a truly personal magic.

The number of this card, the figure and letter "I", is indivisible within the language of the Tarot numbers. *The Magician* stands for that part of personal existence which is indivisibly inherent. To play off his individuality is to achieve his magic.

In your life you are able to accomplish real miracles that surprise others but appear quite natural to you; just as other people succeed in bringing magical things into their own lives that always remain unreachable for you, simply because their way is not yours. Let us have a closer look at this topic.

WHAT DOES THE MAGICAL WAND MEAN?

The Magician is holding a magic wand, and beyond the Tarot, through *Harry Potter* and other stories, we know a lot about these specific sticks. To understand how this magic works in real life, we have to recall the basic elements. There are four classical elements in the Western tradition (and you may have a look at them in the following pages (pp. 62, 84, 108 & 132).

Element	Suit	Basic meaning
Fire	Wands	Action, drive, willpower – catharsis of will
Water	Cups	Feeling, desire, faith – soul and psyche
Air	Swords	Thinking, judging, knowing – intellect, mind, and spirit
Earth	Pentacles	Talents, finances, products – body, matter

Now, if you know the four elements, the symbolic meaning of the magic wand becomes evident. The *Magician connects* two poles in a common whole. And he makes a *distinction* within the One according to two directions.

He is able, for example, to connect fire and water (willpower and feeling) so that the water does not extinguish the fire and nor does the fire evaporate the water. Rather, there is a kind of interaction (e.g. a rainbow). At the same time, he is also able to separate willpower and feeling and keep the advantages and disadvantages within fire and water apart.

THE DEVELOPMENT OF PERSONAL MAGIC

The individual significance of this magic becomes clear when you replace "fire and water" from the example mentioned previously with the real competing demands of your life; those that are important to you personally, e.g. your professional career or spending time together with your children.

Unless you take an individual approach, you won't reach a solution – the wonder of a satisfying combination of both – a fortunate "unity in contradiction." The One has to be separated into two ends (which parts of your career are essential and which

not; which parts of family life are essential and which not). And the requested poles (essential career plus essential family life) are to be linked and united to ONE fitting solution.

To accomplish such a perfect wonder and to keep it current, the Tarot cards offer their step-by step companionship.

AND THIS IS HOW IT'S DONE

Card for the Day

- It's best to begin with the "card for the day." One card is drawn either in the morning or the evening – as the daily topic

Spread Reading

- With your question in mind, shuffle the cards as normal. Hold the cards face down, i.e. with the images downward, and, in a state of relaxation and concentration, draw three cards, one after the other.

- Place the cards face down in front of you in the sequence shown in the pattern of the spread on page 13, Three Cards for the Day.

- Now turn the cards face up, one by one.

- Open your mind to the symbols of the cards. Meditate on their meanings.

- All the cards of this spread together provide the answer or the mirror for today.

- Choose one practical action in consequence, and do it before the next card reading.

If you would then like to try more, choose one of the spreads of several cards (see pages 13-14).

Everyday Spreads

Three cards for the day

1. the current situation
2. the past, or what is already there
3. the future, or something new to be taken into account

Five cards for the day

1. the key, or main factor
2. the past, or what is already there
3. the future, or something new to be taken into account
4. the root, or base
5. the crown, the opportunity, the trend

ALTERNATIVE SPREADS

THE STAR

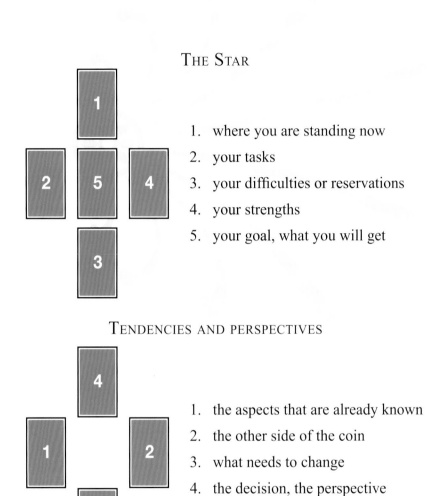

1. where you are standing now
2. your tasks
3. your difficulties or reservations
4. your strengths
5. your goal, what you will get

TENDENCIES AND PERSPECTIVES

1. the aspects that are already known
2. the other side of the coin
3. what needs to change
4. the decision, the perspective

Interpretations for every card

The 22 Major Arcana Cards

I
THE MAGICIAN

THE MAGICIAN

The "magic tools" lie in front of you: The tools and the tasks of your daily life – that's where your magic develops. What can you do? What do you lack? What would you really like to try?

Don't be overly hasty, saying "But I can't do this or that." You have been given the possibility with your universal gifts. The wand is your readiness to experience the whole spectrum of yourself and your opportunities. *The Magician* symbolizes the enchanter who hides in all of us. The magic, the "possibility of the impossible," is being at one with the universe, with God and the world.

The number one is one of the non-divisible numbers in the Tarot. "Non-divisible" in Latin is individuum. As a magician, you are capable of bringing about wonders on your path through life, wonders that are quite natural for you, just as those pieces of magic worked by other people remain inaccessible to you because their way is not your way.

Build upon your ingenuity – the gift of finding yourself and the skill of finding a gap or building a bridge that meets your present requirements. No-one can show you your own personal opportunities and no-one can take them away! They are open only to you.

LOVE A lot of magic lives within us, especially when we are in love. And if we want to fall in love, we "only" have to wake up this magic in us again!

HAPPINESS You are a very special person!

SUCCESS The key to success: Readiness of mind and personal presence!

THE MAGICIAN

II
THE HIGH PRIESTESS

THE HIGH PRIESTESS

The *High Priestess* was once the prophetess, the oracle that could be sought out for advice and aid. This card can mean that it would be good to get advice for your present questions. Basically, however, you can and must help yourself. Read in the "holy book," the book of life, your personal diary! If you want to know whether and how right something is, you have to assess the experiences. Draw upon your experience and the life experience of others, books, etc. And then meditate. It is important that you deal with the inner meaning of your practical action.

Find the best way to help you understand the inner voice: The Tarot cards, for example, but also meditations, dream interpretation, keeping a diary, etc. Study interpretation of feelings, dreams, and intuitions. Take them seriously, but not at face value. Understand their significance. Seize the courage to handle your feelings.

One time it is all about creating a private sphere for yourself, your own room. Another time it is about opening up the walls to the outside in order to exchange feelings.

LOVE Other people's advice or impersonal oracles won't help. Form your own opinion. Perhaps this is also a good opportunity to cry, scream, and sing.

HAPPINESS Happiness in the pure sense of the word: Bury fruitless stubbornness and you will find the *sense of self*, your own meaning!

SUCCESS The key to success: Looking for the deeper meaning, an independent orientation.

THE HIGH PRIESTESS

III
The Empress

THE EMPRESS

The card of Venus – of beauty and love. You can forget any artistic profiling for your present questions. You can also distance yourself from complacency and hypersensitivity.

Don't let yourself be determined by external duties and goals. Handle them, but take care of your responsibility to yourself with respect to your own comfort.

It is often the little things that can make the daily routine diverse and beautiful. You have to use your own creative powers. That is indeed no small matter. It is a question of enjoying life and everyday eroticism. It is about being close to yourself, not fooling yourself and accepting, experiencing, and passing life on to others with love and passion.

Deal with your experiences and perception of femininity. Be a good wife, friend, or mother to yourself and others. Every person embodies a specific truth, which is unique to them and characterizes them. Make your emotions fruitful; defend the people you love!

LOVE When we love and are loved, our personal nature blooms. Where sense and sensibility are given a chance, love grows and, with it, the beauty of being. Speak to people with respect. You will make a huge difference and gain a lot.

HAPPINESS Make yourself comfortable! Support your loved ones.

SUCCESS The key to success: Naturalness and feelings of comfort. Attract what you desire.

THE EMPRESS

IV
THE EMPEROR

THE EMPEROR

The Emperor is the power in all of us to explore new possibilities for life. This figure not only represents government, order, structure, and official power, it is also about self-government, self-determination, and the personal kingdom. In addition, it represents a life principle, being the first to tread and claim new ground.

In this way, The Emperor is also the card of all of us being and remaining "absolute beginners."

You are the master of your actions. You have the responsibility and the freedom to organize and rule yourself. Naturally, this applies to women as well as men! Check your image of masculinity.

Take care and protect yourself from egotism and disinterest. Try being the friend, husband, son, father, etc. that you would like for yourself. To rule yourself means to discover yourself. Risk and enjoy, independently, without a guide and in your own interest.

LOVE You also need power in love – the ability to really bring about something. It is a question of your readiness to get involved and go beyond the boundaries. If you concentrate your energy and power, you can move mountains.

HAPPINESS You are most irresistible when you follow your own spirit and don't settle for half measures or something fake. Use your personal power. "Inside each of us is a king. Call him and he will appear" (Scandinavian saying).

SUCCESS The key to success: Pioneering spirit. Be the leader. You can do it.

V
THE POPE

THE POPE

You have something to say, to convey. You have a unique treasure trove of experience and knowledge within you that others can benefit from. But you can't convert or convince anybody; they have to do that themselves. The other person ultimately makes the decision based on their own experience. However, be generous and demonstrate your treasures. In everything that you do or don't do, you are always an orientation and reference point for others. Everyone is the teacher of everyone else. Express yourself and benefit from the experiences of others.

This card should be understood as a call to make yourself *independent* in questions of faith. What once was the task of the priests and high priests is today a topic for everyone: How can we find personal answers to the great and little mysteries of life? How can we organize those parties and festivities?

You will find your solution if you let others know your secrets and if you let others introduce you into their circumstances. In this way, understanding awakes – and a belief that is not based on dogma or blind trust, but rather on experience.

LOVE Let others know your plans and intentions. And remain open to what others have to say to you.

HAPPINESS The temple of encounter is everywhere. Everywhere, mutual learning and teaching is taking place. It is important that you deal with guides and authorities without haughtiness and with a good feeling of self-esteem.

SUCCESS The key to success: Your own competence. The joy of learning and of teaching.

THE POPE

VI

THE LOVERS

THE LOVERS

The card of love – renewed by daily choice and approval. You don't first need a partner to be strong and reach the peak from which you can "talk to angels." If you expect others to fulfill your wishes and passions, you will make yourself dependent and at the same time prevent yourself from getting involved in deeper and equal relationships and encounters.

At first glance, it is a card of myth and romance. However, the challenging, beautiful path of love means a long process of finding and recognition: "For someone who doesn't understand, mountains are mountains./ For someone beginning to understand, the mountains are no longer mountains./ For someone who understands, mountains are mountains again" (Zen saying).

LOVE You are a loving and loveable person. Say "Yes" to you and those closest to you. Your relationships with others and your relationship with yourself are two sides of the same coin. Don't blame others for your happiness or misfortune. You are always free to make a new decision! When did you last make a declaration of love: to your self – to someone else?

HAPPINESS From a divine point of view, *only he who loves, lives*. Love is not only a feeling. Love is also the decision to look after and really approach another person or circumstance. Love is a state of energy, an existence, which is more beautiful, alive, and richer than a life without love – and therefore it is a direct path to happiness.

SUCCESS The key to success: A renewal of love is waiting for you! Launch yourself into it right now! Just decide.

VII
THE CHARIOT

VII

THE CHARIOT

That you are a headstrong subject is only one side of your existence. The other side is your vehicle of subconscious and unconscious, of animalistic and vegetative energies and forces. You are present in a particular *life-story*, which you can't get out of, and for which you can find only one suitable direction!

The handling of today's drives and needs prepares the way for tomorrow. Where you work on your inner sources and outer goals, the power of *The Magician* confirms this on new levels. You can improve your "Karma" and make your own history.

"You are going the way of the wishes, and that is never easy" (Michael Ende). Which wishes are wise and which not? Which fears are justified and which not? Everything you do is worthwhile as long as you move in this specific way, even if it is perhaps connected with troubles and detours. Conversely, even the greatest achievements remain personally *worthless* if they don't help you progress further on the way of the wishes. And the well-known quotation "The way is the goal" is also valid only in respect to the *way of the wishes*!

> ***LOVE*** Accept and love "yourself and your neighbor," including their own personal strengths and weaknesses. Protect yourself from people who are closed to their inner contradictions. Don't trust one-way streets and similar solutions that are the same for everyone.
>
> ***HAPPINESS*** The way of wishes is the path for fulfilling meaningful desires and dispelling groundless fears – the best path to and in happiness!
>
> ***SUCCESS*** The key to success: Be brave and energetic in dealing with yourself and others.

The "just" and correct handling of libido (drive energy, desire) is, however, in another word – love! Because love is not only a feeling; love is a matter of consciousness, the personal *unity with creation*, with all energies including the self and also completely beyond it.

Love is a decision, an approach to everything there is: "Love in every relationship." The love of creation and all living things is the greatest.

VIII
STRENGTH

Live with the lion in you! You need this exciting prickle and to be at the center of things. If you have a personal relationship with your lions, you have a lot of trust in yourself. You approach problems energetically, and you get what you need. To tame and claim the lions in you means to show what you can do and not hold back. If you commit your energy to the game and can say: "Yes, this is my game," then you embody the powerful joy of one who knows his profession and enjoys it.

We often believe that we have too little energy and need to replenish it like an empty battery. Like the sun, our energy of life is always present, but sometimes it is hidden. See conflicts as challenges that you can deal with in a playfully aggressive manner. They are also rubs and caresses in which everything possible is hidden – closeness, warmth, pulse, pleasure in life, fireworks … And that is exactly the food that your lion needs. "Sometimes my heart stumbles sweat gathers on my brow. Then I think my circulation will give in. But if I stop my circulation my heart jumps as if it were healthy" (Harald Utecht).

LOVE You don't need to be afraid of the acid tests.

HAPPINESS "The beauty and the beast" – they are also you. Happiness is being present as a whole person, collecting and focusing all the strengths at the given moment.

SUCCESS The key to success: Full power – here and now!

IX
THE HERMIT

THE HERMIT

This card represents the necessary phases of conscious loneliness, meditation, immersion in a practical task, abstinence, etc. Withdrawal, quietness, and reflection are not only something for when times are bad. They are at the center of concentration, self-awareness, and reassurance, which you need for your development.

In this, searching and finding are not necessarily the same. Take care to make sure you arrive. Don't forget to find. Start with yourself. The words of St. Francis of Assisi apply in many cases: "What you seek is that which seeks."

Ultimately, this card signifies a high degree of responsibility and reassessment. Cast off obligations – in the material and moral areas. Increase prosperity, well-being and comfortable feelings for yourself and your fellow men.

LOVE "If I attach myself to another person because I cannot stand on my own two feet, he is perhaps my lifesaver, but our relationship is not love. Ironically, the ability to be alone is the pre-condition for the ability to love" (Erich Fromm, The Art of Love).

HAPPINESS *The Hermit* embodies a person who solves his/her problems at the right time and deals with his/her problems without sweeping anything under the carpet. You also have the possibility of making yourself and the world a little bit brighter.

SUCCESS The key to success: Come to terms with yourself.

X
WHEEL OF FORTUNE

WHEEL OF FORTUNE

Your experiences flow together to form your own view of the world. You make your own rhyme to the riddle of life. You hold the power to discover the world further, to wonder and be amazed. Even if everything is turned around, and your previous experiences are reversed, you find the overview, the whole once again. You know your history and your connection, like the sphinx on the wheel. "I live on the crest of a wave. Vulnerable with all my uncertainties – how do you hold on in a river? Indestructible and strong with my feeling that I can continue only in this direction" (Anja Meulenbelt).

Take part in world affairs and the world will take part in you! Turn towards everything you possess – all your strengths and weaknesses – the requirements of the moment.

Protect yourself from breaking down life into individual areas. Sum up your experiences.

LOVE A false romance stimulates illusions – exaggerated generosity, but also exaggerated helplessness. You have to make an appearance and give your commitment to be able to pull the strings.

HAPPINESS You find the greatest support for your intentions through recognition of the facts rather than manipulation. "Happiness is talent for fate" (Novalis).

SUCCESS The key to success: The two powers of being able to examine and identify without blinkers that the things in life that you really want are connected in a special way. The time is ripe now for greater context and better solutions!

WHEEL OF FORTUNE

XI

JUSTICE

Here it is about a transcendent experience that makes it clear to us that it is different, greater than our personal point of view. It is also about the conscious handling of the powers of life, the understanding of passions, the encounter of the godly, which is greater than ourselves. Justice is thus not an abstract principle, but rather the practical question of how we create satisfaction and fulfillment of strong needs and vital aims.

"Our experiences turn quickly into judgments. We keep these judgments in mind although we think they are our experiences. Of course, judgments are not as reliable as experiences. A certain technique is necessary to keep the experiences fresh so that one can derive new judgments from them again and again" (Bertolt Brecht). This "technique" is demonstrated by the "weapons of the mind" (of mind, intellect, and spirit) – i.e. the sword and the scales.

LOVE Choose justice as a form of existence, as the intensity and quality of life. In this way, you contribute to something and will be part of something that is greater than you are. Take care and protect yourself from futile ideas and from violence in the name of justice. Give justice on the various levels of your life a new chance.

HAPPINESS Play fair to thy neighbor as to thyself.

SUCCESS The key to success: Support and criticism – everything in the right measure.

XII
THE HANGED MAN

THE HANGED MAN

The *Hanged Man* has a clear and distinct point of view. Only his standpoint is not the earth but rather the heavenly, transcendental perspective. The heaven symbolizes the spiritual side of life. And also: "Man's mind is his kingdom."

Use the present questions to check your beliefs. Also try once to accept or understand the *opposite* position. Don't play the martyr and don't allow a specific tragedy to be glorified. Examine the reference point of your belief and trust.

When you have checked your belief, don't be afraid of trusting it completely: The greatest feelings are a wise belief and passion!

LOVE Among other things, the XII includes twice the VI; in other words, double *The Lovers* – with all their strengths and weaknesses. It is the card of *passion*. It warns of inappropriate stories of suffering. And it encourages great passions, a complete surrender to love.

HAPPINESS You see the world through new eyes. The opposite of your previous or usual view is also true. You learn a new dimension, which appears crazy at first sight. It is the process of becoming whole or healed. You sense yourself in a new way. It is a more intense, heightened awareness, and you glimpse an alternative, all-embracing reality.

SUCCESS The key to success: Change of awareness. And – it is okay now to let go.

XIII
DEATH

DEATH

You finish what is left over, and separate yourself from the old and obsolete. You experience a cleansing and clarification of your wishes and fears. And you gain a new readiness, a clear openness. When you go through this process, you create space for new opportunities and a new sunrise.

Sadness due to death and loss is unavoidable. But the dreadful fears of a suppressed death are unnecessary and undeserving. You can be dead long before you die. And you can live long after you have died!

And thus, death does not mean nothingness: The reaper wants to harvest something! He wants to bring in the harvest. Therefore, the black rider carries a harvest crown on his standard. Separate yourself from that which is dead, and keep hold of what lives. Decide what is now ripe for harvest and, conversely, where you should make space to sow something new.

The card also addresses your "positive aggression", the power to deal with necessary and far-reaching changes. Your aggressive impulses are only dangerous if you try to deny them.

LOVE Create space for something new, for new opportunities and a new sunrise. You cannot develop your power and might *against* others, *but only* for you.

HAPPINESS "And as long as you do not have, This: Die and be reborn! You are but a dreary guest On this dark earth" (Johann Wolfgang vonGoethe).

SUCCESS The key to success: "Positive aggression" - fight for wise changes.

XIV

TEMPERANCE

There you stand – at the mixing desk of your own personal world. Here it is about temperance, not as frugality or mediocrity, but about the measure of things. Your processing of experiences and impressions reveals itself as a redesign of your everyday life.

The right measure is one of the ancient cardinal virtues. But the image also shows the triumph of wishful thinking, a noble search for ideals, a symbolic or theatrical life. In the separation of desire and reality, of the clear will and the unconscious, real action can occasionally be a crucial test.

Through it, you experience "purgatory": Grasp the contradictions of your life with both hands! Facts can be changed; they are a matter of fact. A creative change during which the previous facts are reforged.

LOVE Through your actions you create new facts – and continuously reinvent yourself. It is important to take care of your partner, but without entering into false compromises.

HAPPINESS The great work – great happiness. Prepare a great work from a given period of life, a *complete art work* of tasks and obstacles, successes and experiments. In doing so, you break the circle of repetition. The creative power leads you to your roots and connects you with the absolute. It is as intimate, as personal, as love. And just as precious.

SUCCESS The key to success: Your creativity, your power to convert and create.

XV

THE DEVIL

THE DEVIL

The spontaneous feeling with this card is often one of being overwhelmed. And not without reason. Don't let yourself be demonized and don't make others the scapegoat. Now is the chance to knock off a pair of old "horns." The *Devil* symbolizes a piece of untouched nature. He embodies things and processes that were previously present only subliminally. Now they cross the threshold.

On the one hand, the *Devil* represents a vampire, a true burden with which we make our own lives and those of others difficult. We are afraid of this with good reason, and can now rid ourselves of this part of the darkness because we recognize it.

On the other hand, the *Devil* embodies a deprived child. It is part of us that we have treated, until now, with neglect, although we long for it. We can now bring it home. If we bring light into the dark, the vampire crumbles to dust and the deprived child takes on form and color.

LOVE Acknowledgment and a practical test for love. Don't let it put the wind up you. Make space for the unknown. It is important to recognize chaotic feelings and chaotic events! Accept unknown experiences but remain true, hold tight and defend what you love and what is sacred to you!

HAPPINESS Meaningless taboos can be cast aside; meaningful taboos can be acknowledged or established!

SUCCESS The key to success: Let go of your preconceptions. Grab the courage to redefine talent and taboos. Bring light into the darkness and you will find new treasures.

XVI
THE TOWER

XVI

THE TOWER

Learn to fly. Think for a minute about parachutists or divers in the swimming pool to understand: It is also a desire and adventure "to fall from the clouds"…

The Tower of Babel and its counterpart – Pentecost: The "Holy Ghost" – comes in the form of tongues of fire around the disciples; they begin to speak, and everyone hears them in their own mother tongue. Instead of confusion, the barriers of language and understanding are lifted.

Babel and Pentecost – two opposite poles using the highest energies that we know. Two completely different ways to be overcome with energy. Violence destroys and leads to speechlessness and confusion. Love, on the other hand, not only breaks down language barriers, it allows understanding across the borders.

LOVE The card of hardening and explosive conflicts. But this is also the image of ecstasy, orgasm, and courage to leave the ivory tower and, at the same time, to remove the masks and open up to love and life.

HAPPINESS Great energy will be released if you advance towards what you really want. "If you have decided for yourself, it's time to let go of some of the Gods" (Ina Deter).

SUCCESS The key to success: Invest in openness and directness! Thus you dare to fly. Try to see this as an experiment that you can perform with trust, confidence, and the readiness to surprise and be surprised. Breathe deeply and open your eyes.

THE STAR

THE STAR

The *Star* is an embodiment of our hopes, but also of every pipe dream that is not so down to earth. The card can represent brazenness as well as the exaggerated search for sensations (star and fan culture): The danger of losing oneself or egocentricity.

"Every life stands under its own star" (Hermann Hesse). Follow your star and you will find your very own source. You will discover the real treasure of your life within you. Allow your personal kind of excellence to emerge, the true beauty and wonderful truth that are hidden in you. Thaw out frozen feelings. Bad experiences need to be worked through and closed, wonderful hopes dreamt to their conclusion and brought to fulfillment!

LOVE The search for the star is the life elixir of every partnership that does not want only to go round in circles and stagnate. Because, from time to time, the path to the great lifetime dream has particular highs and lows, the following is especially true: A trouble shared is a trouble halved – shared joy is double joy!

HAPPINESS Follow your star, which means: Be clear and want your dreams to come true. Don't be put off by the saying "don't reach for the stars."

SUCCESS The key to success: You need to be sharp-witted so that you can evaluate events in context and recognize your path. And you need the courage of unconventionality to leave the trusted paths if you want your desires to lead you to new shores.

THE STAR

XVIII
The Moon

The gate to heaven stands wide open. This is the card of the collective subconscious. Feelings, moods, and attitudes that have characterized the spiritual life of generations and whole continents make an impact. Learn to value and enjoy your connection. Sense your role as part of the flow of life. Swim free like a fish in water.

The *Moon* calls hidden emotions to light, like the crayfish that represents ancient feelings and instincts. Like on a full-moon night, it can be disturbing when the highs and lows of life, which are otherwise hidden slumbering, suddenly become alive. Courage and caution are required here!

The great opportunity consists of recognizing empathy in every living creature. Nothing between the heavens and earth is foreign to you. Accept the great feelings as reality that wants to be experienced just like all other aspects of reality.

LOVE Give your nocturnal side space without surrendering to it. Get to know the "strangers in the night." Become comfortable with them and they with you. Take your partner with you.

HAPPINESS The promise of the card is the redemption of that which was previously suppressed: The lows, like your highs, take shape and are neutralized in everyday life.

SUCCESS The key to success: Find a sensible approach to that which can no longer be calculated and cannot be rationally understood. Take the present wishes and fears seriously and do something with them.

THE MOON

XIX

The Sun

The *Sun* symbolizes regeneration, light and warmth. In general it stands for the all-embracing and central collective conscious (just as the *Moon* stands for the collective subconscious) with which you are at one with the creativity and the general consciousness that other people experience. As soon as we have left childhood, we are consciously working to become a child again and let our own sun shine.

You will find your place in the sun, where you can unfold all your essential assets. Where you can say with full conviction: "This is right!" A creative, rapid unfolding in all directions marks both sunlight and your growth in early childhood. Being a child as an adult means eliminating growth constraints at every age, always doing something new and developing further. What you keep and what you gain is an open dedication to the world. It gives you overwhelming strength, together with a playful pleasure in your existence.

LOVE Always continue to grow, to live consciously, experience consciously and also – age consciously. This opens up a bright perspective for every partnership: *The longer, the better* – this also applies if the relationship develops further and every partner always receives enough sun.

HAPPINESS The happiness of being reborn, dedication to life, in humility and passion, in the knowledge of your place and your path. "The way home is the way forward, the deeper it leads into life" (Colin Wilson).

SUCCESS The key to success: Shake off the labels. "Love God and then do whatever you wish" (St. Augustine aka St. Austin).

XX
JUDGEMENT

From a long way off, we all look the same. In the end, everyone is on their own. Everyone has their own nakedness and needs love. Everyone is only a small part in the large concert of the universe and needs companionship. If you learn to forgive yourself and others again and again, then the old tensions will be released and new possibilities will open up. Hold out your hand for a new beginning, a departure, a reassessment or clarification. If you can draw a line under the past, you will feel reborn. You can always wake up to a new life.

Today is "Judgment Day." Every day is a departure and a new beginning. If you can accept every day as a gift, every day you create new trust and new readiness for life. Longings and fears will always accompany you, but you can learn to handle them. The dark, the pressure, and constriction dissolve and open up.

LOVE Strong forces act upon you, and strong forces are available to you. Today is your day! Everything is important, but you can choose how you handle *everything*.

HAPPINESS Learn to forgive without forgetting. Give yourself and others a new chance.

SUCCESS The key to success: A break from the everyday routine works wonders. Develop guiding principles and visions that suit your real experiences and needs! You have enormous energy reserves. Use them now!

XXI
THE WORLD

THE WORLD

The earth is also made for you. You find yourself at the center, between all the corners of the world, represented here by the four basic elements. You have two wands in your hands: It's not only about combining individual opposites but also about the connection of all four elements, about the combinations of all the possible opposites. Use and design your space in the world.

Nothing can be understood on its own. For every sentence there is an opposite; for every phrase, an objection. The purpose of the dispute with the poles of life is to *live in the now* – develop a personal environment that exploits the abundance of opportunities on offer!

Both "criteria" can and should be grasped: world experience and self-experience, the "intimate circle" of the private, domestic and personal, as well as the "macrocosmos," the public, political and general …

LOVE … This means the man must see the woman in himself to understand the world. And the woman has to see herself in the world to understand herself.

HAPPINESS Take part in the world, and the world will take notice of you. So, the individual life is enriched with universal components; the simple life is at the same time doubled (like the two wands): "*You only live twice!*"

SUCCESS The key to success: Here this is a sign to recognize the time and make your mark. Develop an awareness of your own limits and opportunities.

O
THE FOOL

O

THE FOOL

As a Fool, you travel light – perfectly untroubled. That might seem inviting. But the zero (the traditional number of this card) also warns about a life according to the motto "all talk, no action."

Taken positively, the zero represents the intra-personal interface, the point of internal cohesion, like the origin of a coordinate system: The *beginning and end of everything* that is important for one's own self. Thus, the zero becomes the symbol of the essential and the art of being at home everywhere, because you live at the center. The inner emptiness or calm (see the white sun) allows you to dispense with external models and expectations; at the same time, it experiences the *abundance of life* at and as the center of existence.

This inner emptiness or calm creates a great openness. Thus, connections and *synchronicities* (concurrences) are formed between the individual and the whole.

One such *harmony of man and creation* means at the same time the maximum of personal effectiveness. One cannot achieve and cause more than that. And to do less would be to renounce the existing possibilities.

LOVE Freedom and personal liberty have long been seen as contradictory in stable relationships. But that is far from the truth! Two *Fools* in love are also the two *zeros* that together form a *lemniscate* – a lying-down figure eight, which is the sign of eternity and is also very similar to the conventional wedding symbol.

HAPPINESS Only fulfillment of the basic wishes and the handling of important fears make you perfectly happy in the pure sense of the words.

SUCCESS The key to success: One can also call it the "Forrest Gump Principle": being in the right place at the right time.

INTERPRETATIONS FOR EVERY CARD

THE 56 MINOR ARCANA CARDS

ACE OF WANDS

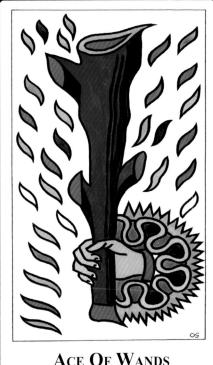

ACE OF WANDS

First and foremost, the wand is a phallic symbol, even if this is barely mentioned in Tarot books (but all the more in the literature on interpreting dreams). Sexuality, potency, and phallic power not only belong "to it," they are the embodiments of the powers of fire. As a phallic symbol, it signifies the energies of men. But not only of men: The motif of the witch's broom in myths and fairytales and the image of the *Queen of Wands* also know the wand as part of the power of women.

The fire gives you the power of drives, the flames of vitality, and the dynamics of will. The hand emerging from the cloud: That you are rediscovering the fire once again and can take it in your hand is a gift of life. The will to be yourself and the desire to surpass yourself represent the two poles of a wand. Contribute to banishing the human cold, colorlessness and "inactivity" back to where they belong, like the powerless yet violent powers of fire that aimlessly wander the earth.

> **LOVE** Sexuality, adventure, life with children and the elderly (and also with the inner child and the wise elder in yourself) – every type of creativity encourages the artistic use of fire …
>
> **HAPPINESS** … and with it, you will spin straw into gold.
>
> **SUCCESS** Don't let anybody force the law of action upon you. You remain at the helm.

Two Of Wands

Two Of Wands

Desire and burden of the beginning: The art of being able to start something with many people, tasks, and energies. This card is about the great energy that you need and that you gain when you distribute your energies into viable steps and steer towards the great goals.

The wands mean driving force, zest for life and the need for self-development. The *Two of Wands*, therefore, represents polarity, which can mutually block and strengthen. How do you cope with the opposing motives and goals – with important interests and intentions that are controversial within your own person or between yourself and others?

Don't let yourself be driven into a life of permanent stress. Avoid bigotry, and apply your true ardor. Something new is developing in your present questions, which only you can discover. A world is at your command, just do it smoothly.

LOVE Energy work – reluctant drives and overlapping interests must be managed skilfully, especially in a partnership. This is less a topic for discussion than it is a mature consideration and action.

HAPPINESS Only one who can also be a beginner can master their profession.

SUCCESS Wait until you have a rounded view of things and you have made a decision. Then don't hesitate any longer! Act with all your power.

THREE OF WANDS

You are a powerful, deep-rooted personality. Your wealth of ideas, energies, and momentum combine with your sense of adventure and readiness to move something. The card stands for solid work. And it stands for the many goals that you still foster inside you, the joy of new enterprises.

It can say to you: What are you still waiting for? What should you be afraid of? Get on with it! An idea is only as good as what you make out of it. Look forward. Rely on the power and integrity of your plans. Set sail for new shores.

The strengths and weaknesses of this powerful card depend on whether the existing contradictions are acknowledged or suppressed. The subconscious plays a part. To avoid a feeling of aimlessness or helplessness ("for they know not what they do"), it depends on living consciously and paying careful consideration to the reverse sides of people and events.

THREE OF WANDS

LOVE Now is a good time for you to bring color into your everyday life and to get to know new people. Others will also approach you full of energy. But don't rush. Look carefully at their suggestions.

HAPPINESS "If you know what you are doing, you can do what you want" (Moshé Feldenkrais).

SUCCESS Stay patient and firm in your will. Don't allow obstacles to block you, but instead let them stimulate you!

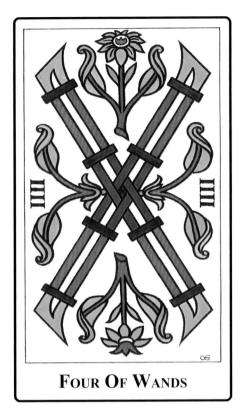

FOUR OF WANDS

FOUR OF WANDS

A card of strong energy! We don't find magical "places of power" only at particular natural areas or magical sites. We encounter the wonder of creation everywhere in principle, and meet our most intimate – most difficult and most beautiful – experiences. Birth, wedding and death always push us to the limits – and to the center of our existence.

And in these sometimes shocking, often wonderful, but always amazing experiences, the need for culture awakes – the incentive to express and process what moves us, through play, music, and dance!

Celebrations and cultural events can give us wings or "distract" us so that we can hardly find ourselves again. The higher we advance in life, the more it's a matter of sensing (again) what moves us inwardly to deepen our own self-conception.

LOVE Show yourself as the man or woman that you are. Your sexual identity is an indispensable source of energy.

SUCCESS Don't commit yourself to compromises as far as your basic convictions and personal truths are concerned!

HAPPINESS Avoid messy solutions. Don't hide your true motivations and real feelings. They provide the best motivations and guarantee the greatest successes!

FIVE OF WANDS

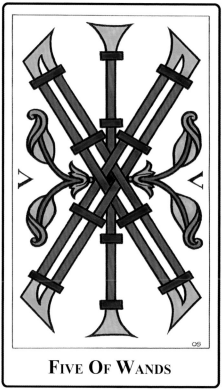

FIVE OF WANDS

This card symbolizes the game, fight, or competition of different energies, from emerging new interests and intentions and also from inside the person him or herself. Only when many flames are metaphorically burning, does the personal will re-form and stay alive.

At the same time, it's also a culture of games, but this means more than the cultivation of party and parlor games. Don't object to it. Here the topic is *taking the whole of life as a game, without gambling it away*. It begins with recognizing your will as something less fixed. Fire is extinguished without movement, and the personal will become exhausted without change.

Your will forms and passes and rearranges itself with every moment, and the image shows us this in a snapshot. The youths represented here mean that it is particularly those developing renewable drives in you that are involved in the present conflict and reformulation of your will.

LOVE You are open to the game of powers – in you, with you, and around you.

HAPPINESS You let yourself by calmed by people, ideas, and events in your environment. Play with them and feel the energy. You can use external and also "opposing" energies for your purposes, like in a creative Aikido or exchange of blows.

SUCCESS Don't let yourself be bullied or hide yourself away. Decide what goals you want to achieve: Make a clear decision and push it through. Half measures will destroy you in the long run.

Six Of Wands

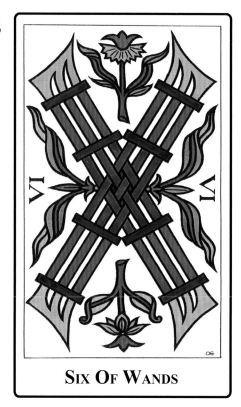

Six Of Wands

The wands are well structured in this picture. So, you are to look for a good outcome of your fiery energies, your willpower, and your actions.

You already have many situations behind you on your journey: a lot of work, a lot of effort, disappointments and acknowledgments. Now you learn that you are on the right track.

You develop your optimum power when you use both strengths and weaknesses together. Act and don't sell yourself short. But also don't hide your "little" weak points. On the contrary, if you follow what you have a weakness for, this will also strengthen you! If you use and count your strengths and weaknesses, your efforts are rewarded, and you remain flexible and can react "holistically."

For your present questions, there are, therefore, only complex answers, no simple or one-dimensional solutions. Complex questions broaden the scope and extent of your possibilities.

Represent what moves you internally and dedicate yourself to it completely. Protect yourself from false heroism that isn't interested in weaknesses. Avoid, also, false shyness and powerless modesty, which don't expect anything from your own strengths.

LOVE Show your strengths and weaknesses, in love and sexuality, too.

HAPPINESS Follow what you have a weakness for and defend your innermost convictions. Then you are on a roll: Unstoppable!

SUCCESS Don't let yourself be bullied and don't place others under pressure!

Seven Of Wands

This represents new energies: Acting for the sake of it and ambition are only damaging right now. A new level is decisive, an "intelligent" style of using energy.

Goal and reward: You achieve more if you wear yourself out a little bit. It is amazing, and it is wonderful! And yet it's nothing incomprehensible; the explanation is right at hand: Just as with school homework, computer languages or the daily routine that we master as adults as a matter of course but which were inconceivable for us as children, in the same way we can achieve a suitable aplomb when handling complex energies and many simultaneous tasks.

Seven Of Wands

But what we can learn from children is again to handle a situation playfully. Just as children can play, completely concentrating on something then moving on in the next moment, and then starting again, always with 100% attention, with enthusiasm, no inner pressure.

LOVE You overcome despondency and blind enthusiasm and don't rely on dramatic decisions and acts of defiance.

HAPPINESS You react to particular challenges with care and high precision and not with stress or tension.

SUCCESS Don't allow yourself to be provoked and don't provoke others! Find a standpoint that emphasizes your sovereignty and permanently preserves your power.

EIGHT OF WANDS

EIGHT OF WANDS

The card represents successful "energy transfer," the ability to move others and let yourself be moved. Your efforts give results. These present you with new challenges. You have many powers, and many things now have to be brought to a new conclusion. A challenging situation that is very demanding of you also threatens to be dangerous in that you completely lose track of yourself.

Make yourself inwardly ready to take a large step. Only you can make your dreams reality. "Take your broken wings, and learn to fly. All your life you were only waiting for this moment to arise: Fly!" sing the Beatles in their song "Blackbird." Have the courage to advance with a broad front on new experiences and impressions.

But at the same time, it is also the card of projections and jugglery. Projections are a heightened form of wishful thinking. One shifts the inner emotions and personal motives to the outside – one's own feelings and needs are seemingly mirrored back at oneself from the outside, like ghosts or as visible objective circumstances. This takes place less in your head as in your stomach and feelings, like a film you take part in without knowing it. Self-checking and external control are most desirable.

LOVE End the unwanted state of uncertainty. Let your senses fly! You can't realize your dreams in a dream.

HAPPINESS Recognize colors and realize the magician hiding in you!

SUCCESS You will gain a wide range of support.

NINE OF WANDS

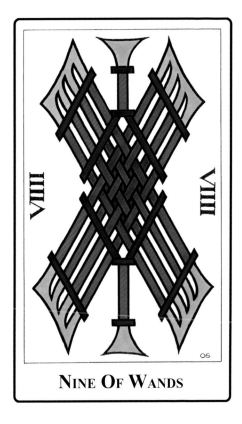

NINE OF WANDS

What is happening? The watchful consideration and examination of all the drives and motivations at work requires and conveys an intuition that is whole and protective. And you will need the power of intuition to be able to choose the right "wand" in any given situation, that is, to give special emphasis to the most urgent matters.

Intuition produces a fine sense of both the visible and invisible details of events. Take remote experiences and events into account, too. Keep an eye on all important developments in your questions and take care of the most urgent things!

Keep your eyes and ears open, but relax at the same time so that you can pay attention to *everything*. Don't listen to rumors; be skeptical of speculations and mere assertions.

LOVE Your current solutions involve living more vitally and getting more from life.

HAPPINESS One step at a time: Get rid of unfounded fears, fulfill important wishes!

SUCCESS Undivided attention for all – strong-hearted action for the most urgent.

Ten Of Wands

TEN OF WANDS

Don't use "a lot" of energy, but all your energies! This is the card of adventure, and, interestingly, it is at the same time, the card of home-coming. There is also this connection in the language: "Adventure" stems from the Latin verb *advenire* – to arrive. Adventure means arrival. Welcome to life!

This represents the totality of the fiery energies of drive, action, willpower, and personal creation. The more you act and do, the more you will have to see to it that you also arrive at yourself. Find your tasks in this life that give you the chance to grow and be in phase with your development during a long lifetime. Think about this and make your current decisions according to your long-term will. Wherever you are able to transfer all of your powers into reality and make "a hundred flowers" bloom, there you will find your home, no matter where you happen to stay.

Only when you give the person, the situation, the questions, etc. your undivided attention can you understand their own logic. You have to lean forwards, dare to set off and completely let go. Then you're ahead. But if you feel that you have taken on too much, throw off the ballast and start again, whatever the matter!

LOVE Use all your energies. Let "a hundred flowers bloom."

HAPPINESS Your commitment is required. Give all that you have!

SUCCESS Don't give up until you have really exhausted all your possibilities.

PAGE OF WANDS

PAGE OF WANDS

The *Page of Wands* (or "knave") is mostly seen as a typical *young* person whose *drive is stronger than his life experience*. It's about novel experiences. Zest for life and the desire to grow present you now with the task of surpassing yourself.

In doing so, the page is either "on guard" and wary of his fire, or his flames engulf him and "go too far." He doesn't realize his own focus, like someone with a crush on his "flame," an idol, or someone who doesn't know what he's doing. Regardless of how old you are or how you feel, protect yourself in the present questions from pointless zealousness and desires which will lead you nowhere.

New propositions offer you new challenges, chances, tests, and acknowledgments. Hold on to what keeps your heart beating!

Don't necessarily measure what now develops as new using previous experiences. Youthful seriousness will now help you best – no matter how old you are. Avoid superficiality and unnecessary dramatization. Thus you stay *young at heart*.

LOVE Understand the energies that are greater than you yourself. Follow your passions in a respectful and sovereign way.

HAPPINESS Take care and protect yourself from bigots.

SUCCESS Keep an eye on your desires and the hour of grace – grab it.

KNIGHT OF WANDS

KNIGHT OF WANDS

With the wand in the very desert this means a "desert" life or the art of changing a desert into a garden, life tasks that are so large that you can use all your energies to accomplish them.

Come out of yourself while considering losses but without particular expectations or pre-judgments. Keep moving. The significance of people and events will become clear to you when something happens.

The *Knight of Wands* does not pass through the fire, but rather he lives at the heart of the fire. A good intuitive ability to react now will help you further, as will a trusting, determined look ahead.

LOVE For women, this often means assuming the leadership themselves. They have to lead themselves and accept the responsibility. For men, this is often about becoming more sensitive to the contradictions of their own person and those of others. They must understand that every contradiction that they notice and react to strengthens them.

HAPPINESS You involve yourself in all the sides of your personality. You act holistically and with every sense, and through acting, you recognize which path is right for you.

SUCCESS Apply yourself fully. Understand what you and others are looking for! You have immense energies, and great tasks and adventures are waiting for you.

QUEEN OF WANDS

QUEEN OF WANDS

The huge scepter clarifies the *Queen of Wands* as an energetic person. As she sits there, majestic, legs spread apart and alert, she gives the impression of self-assurance and being ready to act. She has confidence and approaches life with absolute openness. And therefore she finds herself in a seemingly impossible situation.

With the flower in the desert, either she makes it clear that she has no base, no roots for her blossoming life power and needs to find water as quickly as possible so that her blooming grandeur is not lost, or she is standing in front of a task or has a power that otherwise only the *Emperor* possesses: To change a desert into a garden!

LOVE Your present questions need passion and awareness, a special faith in yourself. As a woman, it is about not leaving the phallic and heroic powers to the men, but rather exerting your own power according to the motto "a witch's broom sweeps well." As a man, you must find the wild cat inside yourself and learn to ride the tiger.

HAPPINESS Show what you are capable of. Determine your own life goals and preserve your pleasure in life!

SUCCESS Be prepared for a phase of heightened activity. Divide your activities and emphasis at every step.

King Of Wands

King Of Wands

This card represents the mastery of fire. You must and you can resist and shape the trials by fire. Even more: You need them. Because dead ballast can be burnt in fire; the slag separates off and the precious material emerges. Your will experiences death and rebirth. If you fundamentally accept trials by fire, you can protect yourself better from unhealthy stress.

Let yourself be challenged and prove yourself! Bury futile vanities and show your strength! You need the energies of this King when you have to master seemingly overwhelming events. What looks huge and overwhelming at first glance will become small with time and will finally turn out to be manageable for you. You only have to wait until the time is right and then proceed with biting wit, like "Puss in Boots" in the fairytale, who first asks the great magician to turn himself into a mouse so that he can catch him and devour him.

LOVE It can be especially important to act independently as a woman and not to fear "death and the devil." As a man, it is important to check what purpose you are really interested in.

HAPPINESS Accept the tasks and challenges of the moment. Take hold, don't pull away at the decisive moment.

SUCCESS You also confront dull aggression and a false heroism best when you go fully through fire for what you love!

ACE OF CUPS

ACE OF CUPS

The *Ace of Cups* contains the whole potential of the spiritual life, the world of feelings and spirituality. This signifies your deep spiritual connection with life and your openness to secrets between heaven and earth. It signals a happy journey through life and deep fulfillment.

Your feelings let you experience joy and pain. You appear to be at the mercy of wishes and fears, which sometimes threaten to engulf you. Sometimes you don't know what is dream and what is reality, where the illusion begins and where it ends. At the same time, it is exactly these extreme emotional experiences that connect you most intensely with the world and what is human.

Also look at the unknown spiritual side. This can sometimes be connected with inner excitement or outward tension. It's not the case that feelings always have to be only "nice" and pleasant. Furthermore, a single cup can naturally also carry the widest range of different elixirs: water and wine, champagne and soda, poison, medicine or a magical potion.

LOVE Discard accountability for your feelings – without censure or pre-evaluation. Now is not the right time for large promises but rather for personal honesty.

HAPPINESS You have a soul with its own name, which expresses your connection with all living things and, at the same time, your characteristics as an individual.

SUCCESS Be ready to forgive yourself and/or others so that it is possible to start again spiritually.

Two Of Cups

Two Of Cups

Happiness and fulfillment between (two) people. Love, understanding, readiness to communicate and exchange are the basis for emotionally satisfactory, happy relationships and encounters; a type of magic is found in such encounters.

The two depicted branches symbolize the body and psyche, drive and reason, sympathy and antipathy. It is your task to separate and discern and re-combine your feelings and emotions. Accept mixed emotions, but if you feel inner stress, then reset your emotional behavior.

Furthermore, there is the question of how to fill your cup. Maybe you see your partner as the "*better half*," and yet you will be continually disappointed until you finally discover the missing part in yourself and become open to others for their own sake and not as an extension or mirror of your own goals!

Take care of your own worries, wishes, and fears. Learn also to distinguish between matters of feelings. The clearer the difference between the partners, the more fruitful are the similarities.

LOVE Everyone has the right to choose and decide for themselves, particularly in emotional and intimate questions.

HAPPINESS One of the reasons for our "long journey through this short life" is the *joy* that we discover in ourselves and share with others.

SUCCESS Tell others what you would like to give them and what you hope to receive.

THREE OF CUPS

THREE OF CUPS

This card is about clearing, differentiation, and the transformation of your personal "cups," the vessels and the tools of feeling, desire, and faith.

It is a constellation into which you are fully accepted and to which you give yourself fully; not to forfeit or sacrifice yourself, but rather out of the pleasure of existing, the desire to give. Those moments in your life in which you have a happy understanding of the world, when a moment is a lifetime, those are the situations of pure bliss in which everything is possible.

Here we see the art of combining feelings and moods. This card is one of the best of the Tarot if we see it as an image of overflowing, fruitful feelings, a rich and fulfilled life. However, the card also warns us of emotional and inner dependency. It represents not only agreeableness but also spiritual arrogance.

Don't depend on the approval of others to validate your feelings. Accept the feelings of others, even if you can't identify with them.

LOVE: Don't be afraid of "emotional" reactions. But sort out your feelings. Approach others, or stay away from them, even if this appears unusual. Your spirit can accept several truths at the same time. Let your spirit grow.

HAPPINESS: Everybody is a beautiful person if you find his/her inner truth.

SUCCESS: Success is also a matter of feelings. In addition, feelings need emotional intelligence so that we might move beyond them and learn the lessons they hold for us.

Four Of Cups

Four Of Cups

Let your spirit wander. Meditate or get rid of what is stopping you meditating or being calm. At peace, you find the words to express experiences and tasks that have long been without language. What were your original goals? It's also about balancing your spiritual experiences and expectations.

Look inside you to overcome what has previously happened and open yourself up to new things. Something has been neglected and wants to be taken care of now. Something now needs processing inwardly. Although this card clearly recommends holding back, sleeping and dreaming enough, the overall signs don't point to withdrawal, but rather to reflection upon your own great opportunities.

Don't become melancholic. Melancholy is the wrong self-will. It dulls the senses. Do exactly the opposite, do what activates and calms the senses and lets them fly. You are offered unusual opportunities, and these are the offer of the day!

LOVE Relax, reflect deeply and reach for new heights. The fourth cup stands for new sights and invitations - which you can accept or reject.

HAPPINESS The encounter with nature gives you deep peace and inspiration. Learn and enjoy being with yourself and listen to your inner flow.

SUCCESS Let your spirit fly. Don't demand or expect anything particular, be open to inspirations. That is most fruitful.

FIVE OF CUPS

FIVE OF CUPS

The quintessence of the cups: We can learn from our own and others' truths and let our love, our soul, grow. Through this we shall experience times of change and transformation again and again.

Offer yourself and others the "plain truth"! It is better to learn the truth "late" than never at all. A disappointment always offers the chance to cast off a delusion; this means taking leave of illusions and starting again with new clarity.

When we start a new chapter in our life-story, we often encounter dark dreams or gloomy feelings. The soul acts like a mirror; but what can the psyche do when there is no image to reflect yet? Indeed, for what's really new our soul has nothing other than darkness – due to the lack of inner images or impressions from our own experience! Such intuition, dark dreams and the like can be a serious warning signal of an unusual danger; then you should immediately seek help. Conversely, however, the spiritual black-out can indicate the beginning of something completely new and positive. These encounters with the unknown give a real feeling of happiness, just like the first glimpse of land after a long voyage at sea.

LOVE Don't run away from your feelings! Cry, but also with happiness. Get help when you need it. Be ready to give help and support. Let it flow.

HAPPINESS Give yourself time and space for inner renewal.

SUCCESS At the end of a phase, when you have learnt the lesson, enormous amounts of energy are released.

Six Of Cups

Six Of Cups

The cups are well structured in this picture. So, you are to look for a good flow for your feelings, your desires, and your life-plans. Work with all resources and get them in a good order. Realize and appreciate being part of something bigger than yourself.

Open yourself to memories, dreams, and inspirations, even if they only appear to involve minor things. Take care when handling emotional experiences. What was good at the time and what not? How can the good things of the past be good again today? How can the bad things of the past be prevented today? Today, you have many different ways of dealing with wishes and fears.

Distinguish between your feelings. And take your time to resolve complex impressions and experiences by clearing them layer by layer!

LOVE This is the right occasion to investigate memories, for instance, by digging out old photographs and notes. Take care of (your) children. Support the inner child in you! Do away with childish reactions and do what you've wanted to do for a long time as a grown woman or man!

HAPPINESS Use this favorable time to dispel old fears and fulfill your heart's desires! It is the right time to dig deeper.

SUCCESS Success comes from your openness to pleasant surprises: Large and small wonders that we must perceive in everyday life.

Seven Of Cups

Seven Of Cups

One of the remarkable qualities of the soul is the ability to expand and outgrow itself. This card is about to what extent this is advisable.

Your crucial task now is to find out which dreams and which fears are really essential for you. Find out at which points you must not give in or give up – and when, conversely, a little less would be more and better!

Thus, there is nothing left but to subject your existing needs and personal goals to scrutiny. Sometimes the greatest longing and most "unrealistic" cravings are just the right desires. In other cases, even the smallest temptation and most harmless promises are evil.

LOVE Examine the root of your fears and follow the desires that release the strongest energy. Develop and represent your own benchmark, particularly in matters of love and intimate desires.

HAPPINESS The enemy of good is the best. Understand and learn the "language of the heart" as you would do any other language – spend time with it, and enjoy the lessons.

SUCCESS Attend to the emotions that occupy your thoughts most often. Explore those that can help you to progress now.

Eight Of Cups

Eight Of Cups

The eight cups are a great wealth of life really lived, of the multitude of experiences and results achieved. However, you must continue onwards now. Standing still would put even the results already gained at risk. Here it is also about feelings that are so great that we can no longer hold the individual cups in our hand, feelings that pull and carry us.

Sometimes the card encourages us to make fluid again those things that have become blocked or even solidified; tears and drink will do us good then. And sometimes it is important to "dry up," look oneself in the face and set oneself a goal. Anyway, the solution here is to free yourself – from inner dependences of whatever kind, so that "it" can flow!

It is not easy to leave the comfort zone. But perhaps it is time to turn away from achievements and habits that may have a particular outcome but don't offer real pleasure. A new start can bring you the experience that it is fun to set yourself in motion again and to feel the vitality within and around you.

LOVE Free yourself of emotional half measures. Everything flows. Nothing is certain except that you are continuing on your path. Thus, you will feel safe and taken care of in this world.

HAPPINESS Hopes and fears lead you on to the source of your longing.

SUCCESS If you follow the flow (the inner slope), at the same time you will get up and achieve new heights in real life. We overcome obstacles and reach new heights if we let the flow guide our actions.

NINE OF CUPS

NINE OF CUPS

How lucky when "all the fountains flow." We are often afraid of our feelings. However, you can't live by permanently ignoring your feelings – they'll get you eventually. But what is in the cups? It is often said, "rely on your gut feeling!" But there are also unreliable feelings or inappropriate inspirations!

You have to decide what is wise and what isn't. Only with conscious review and consideration of the spiritual needs of everyone involved can you progress with your present questions.

LOVE Have the courage to make a decision! Don't let yourself be put off by embarrassment or fascinated by details. Stay true to yourself and "sometimes dance to a different tune"! Then you will gain a richness of great feelings without unpleasant side effects.

HAPPINESS You accept yourself with faults and merits. You are a darling of fortune: Contentedness, pleasure, peace, and harmony grow in you out of your active acceptance of life and your experiences. Trust yourself. "Everything about you is valuable if you just take it into your possession" (Sheldon B. Kopp).

SUCCESS Strength is found in peace. Live the grand emotions – nothing human is foreign to you and none of your most important needs are left unfulfilled! Play the whole instrument of emotions and needs! You can develop in many directions without constant assessment and evaluation and achieve truly pleasing successes.

TEN OF CUPS

TEN OF CUPS

You live with great passion. You rise up and fulfill your life. But be aware of "elevated" pipe dreams and illusions! The plenty of cups can also be negative and represent delusion – a passion creating pain.

From the positive side, the card signifies wonderful experiences and events. The totality of your emotional and psychic "cups" offers the gift of creativity, of the productive lifting of (personal) opposites of every kind!

Then you are like a force field in which you and others feel good. The art is to trust yourself, to risk a way of life that develops every source and makes it fruitful.

LOVE Trust yourself and others; have confidence in yourself and others; entrust yourself and others with something; be in alliance with many and associate with few; enter into a bond of life with everything and all that moves your heart!

HAPPINESS You experience joy, as you do when accepting gifts, but in fact it is the result of your readiness to be open and receive. "See the world in a grain of sand/ and heaven in a wild flower,/ hold infinity in the palms of your hand/ and eternity in an hour" (William Blake).

SUCCESS Your wishes become real in a colorful, kaleidoscope life. You find love and relationships that fulfill you completely. Understand what others say – and what they really mean. Your readiness to be creative in relationships and situations fulfills your longings.

Page Of Cups

PAGE OF CUPS

A wonderful card for summery cheerfulness – at any time of year! Through your feelings you discover new things. You understand the content of the spiritual world, emphasized by the image of the fish understanding the contents of the water world.

This card represents the fertility of spiritual life. And it warns of both unfounded fears and hopes.

LOVE You are a cheerful and serious personality, helpful and constructive, while being independent and self-reliant. You observe the life of feelings and the subconscious with a contemplative youthfulness and curious reservation. As long as that doesn't lead to indecisiveness, you have a great gift for raising inner problems without drowning in them.

HAPPINESS You discover new things and gain important insights through empathy, understanding, and meditation. For you that is a source of enlightened pleasure in life. And you can be a great help to others in the psychic and spiritual area. With your reflective and full-of-life manner, you can fill yourself and others with courage.

SUCCESS We often think that we first need success for life to be light and pleasant. This card, however, suggests the opposite way: Make your life light and pleasant – make sure there is relief from important personal wishes and/or fears. Then you'll also have the desired success.

Knight Of Cups

Knight Of Cups

You are a loving person, upright, straightforward, open. You are riding for love. You follow your great feelings and desires. The *Knight of Cups* reminds us of the quest for the Grail and the courtly love of the age of chivalry. He draws practical conclusions from his feelings. Your present questions require just such conclusions. In any case, you owe yourself a specific emotional straightness.

This card represents an exhilarating attitude to life but also the danger of escaping into a dream world. So you have to clear your beliefs by checking all relevant experiences, both yours and those of others. Your beautiful dreams will come true, if you help yourself.

LOVE Your great love for life is typical of you. You simply have so much love to give. You share yourself and bring laughter and lightness to your surroundings. Be happy and continue like this.

HAPPINESS You can be an outspoken joker. The other side is your great search and traveling. You always need the feeling of being reconnected to your source, of expanding into the infinite and of a deep sense of being at one with the flow of life. Unless you fall into indecision or absent-mindedness, you have an extraordinary gift for wonderful love stories, spiritual adventures, and fantastic experiences. Desires and feelings open up together for you.

SUCCESS Check what you believe and whom you trust. Use your heart and head to experience deep-lying and uplifting feelings: They will show you the path to success.

QUEEN OF CUPS

QUEEN OF CUPS

The loving Queen of the Water: No other Tarot figure embodies the preciousness of feelings quite like this image. Your current questions require courage to feel.

The reality of the soul is a reality like any other. Let it make itself felt in all questions of daily life with the same naturalness, with the same clarity. This often depends on listening to this emotional reality. If you don't grasp your own cup and clearly recognize its value and its limitations, you either won't find an individual reference point or you will deliver your own inner certainty and self-evaluation into others' hands!

LOVE You know a lot of life's secrets and sense them deeply. Your great empathy gives you rich and fitting images, ideas, and visions. You have good antennae, an ear for the subconscious, the "eternal human essence," and the emotions of the soul. You can love with all your heart and share deep feelings. The basis for this is only your openness; this means your art, above all, of accepting what has happened, a significance, a sense.

HAPPINESS If you are aware of who you are, you can draw from it immense power and a fruitful fantasy. In that way you can bring about a deep, beautiful and fulfilled life, with pleasant surprises, heartfelt joy, and always with newly experienced bliss. You are skilled at relationships, a spiritual gift and an experienced worldly wisdom. You thaw many frozen souls.

SUCCESS Decide by listening to your heart. Check the feelings of everyone involved. Clearly represent your point of view.

KING OF CUPS

KING OF CUPS

This card represents mastery of the water element of feeling, desire, and faith. In your current questions, go to the bottom of your feelings (and the feelings of all those involved). Pay attention to deep-seated needs and have the courage to discover your most intense longing and express it. Do not look for strength or even subordination to others in order to even out your own uncertainties. Instead, utter your vague fears and subliminal desires and bring them into your mind and into your communication. Understand that your self-esteem and your longing is your scepter!

LOVE You are a loving, dignified personality, whose great power comes from deep within. Your inner life and feelings are very decisive for you. Until you recognize this, you may seriously damage yourself. But as soon as you follow the impulses of your subconscious and live accordingly, you will be afloat again and will find an expert, hearty way of life "good tempered like a pasha and as vicious as a porcupine" (Italo Calvino).

HAPPINESS You are sensitive to waves and vibrations. The water world with all its depths is your happiness. All the external frameworks (fulfillment of duties, tasks, rules) will not do better.

SUCCESS Protect yourself from personal impositions, but don't be afraid to "go into the depths" and keep things running smoothly. Examine the motives thoroughly – your fine sense of emotions and instincts leads you to many, often brave, ideas and inspirations, which will bring you to your goal.

ACE OF SWORDS

ACE OF SWORDS

The Ace of Swords stands for intellectual energy in the pure, concentrated form. It's about the electricity that lets the thoughts sizzle, the crown of creation or, on the other hand, a maximum estrangement from nature.

Everything has its proverbial two sides, and this is very appropriate for the double-edged sword.

Take it as a gift and duty to grasp the sword anew, to find new solutions and make new decisions! The spirit through which everything flows also creates universality and unity. It is a prejudice that the spirit only brings about separation.

LOVE Like an eagle, you see things clearly and sharply as individuals as well as in combination. The card signifies a genuine, free security that you partly already possess and partly have yet to achieve.

HAPPINESS Perceive the spirit that lives inside us all and flows throughout you! Starting to think again brings you happiness. The fruitfulness of the intellect is measured in its elevation, refinement, and the fulfillment of needs – that is the benchmark.

SUCCESS Stand up, straighten up, and enjoy a new clarity. For your present question, this card means heightening your consciousness, sharpening the contradictions and finding a denominator. Ensure a unity of thought and action. Free yourself of inappropriate doubts and ambiguities.

TWO OF SWORDS

TWO OF SWORDS

Balance the weapons of the intellect; open your mind. Understand and explore the unknown. Be aware of the boundary *between* day and dream, between sleeping and waking. Keep this crossing open. It's no use barricading yourself or blocking the entrance to the feelings.

As soon as you can sort out the feelings and fantasies, you will gain insight into areas that extend far beyond mere vision. Like a radio operator who has made contact with a distant continent, you gain insight and understanding of the life-and-soul areas stretching far beyond your own area of experience.

LOVE Look behind the curtain. It is better to interpret feelings and dreams, to "digest" experiences. The more clearly you understand the difference between fantasy and reality, the easier it will be for you to find peace. The reward will be new pleasure and lightness in the partnership.

HAPPINESS Ambivalence, ambiguity, and contradiction are part of life. You don't allow yourself to be discouraged by the abundance of different experiences and don't hide behind indecision or flattery.

SUCCESS Bring your fantasy into play, and success will be by your side. There is no absolute right or wrong, only what is right for you just now. Do what you have to do, and be ready to learn from your past and your future experiences.

THREE OF SWORDS

THREE OF SWORDS

This card is about clearing, differentiation, and the transformation of your personal "swords." This means the weapons and the tools of intellect, mind, and spirit.

The "three swords" are often misunderstood as the "heartache card." Indeed, it does concern the heart and mind finding a new unity. The known and the unknown, conscious and subconscious, external arguments and inner experience, are to be separated, valued, and connected with each other.

LOVE If you draw this card, you can stop fooling yourself and others. Risk more honesty. You can only win by doing so. Speak frankly. This is the hour of truth. You are offered a special chance to understand what lies behind the oppositions and contradictions. There is a wonderful new solution, and you slowly recognize it.

HAPPINESS Explore the power of veracity. Don't let yourself be paralyzed by problems or difficulties, and don't get into a rage. There are unavoidable difficulties that we all have to cope with and avoidable mistakes that we can correct. In particular, the power to clear away problems and mistakes lies within the great, fruitful, and comforting power of the spirit. Use it!

SUCCESS Come to the point, keep to what is important. If you know what moves your partners deep down inside, you can start doing what really is essential.

FOUR OF SWORDS

05

FOUR OF SWORDS

This card is about checks and balances concerning your own and others' experiences. On the one hand, the four swords show a truce or a deadlock or an interregnum. On the other hand, these symbols stand for peace, inner composure, deliberateness, and maturity.

It shows that you have done and experienced a great deal, which you now have to air. It is possible that important events are ahead of you, like a musician or sportsman who has practiced the exercise a hundred times over but still needs to concentrate and gear himself up each time.

In principle, this card is not concerned with outer calm but rather with spiritual peace. It's about personal contentment and inner peace.

LOVE Don't become a victim to lifeless ideals. You feel light and alive with a clear conscience. Peace of mind will make you free from illusions. This opens the door to a new kind of love.

HAPPINESS Contemplation, reflection, and meditation are important for your happiness. Your self-chosen distance from everyday confusion allows inner knowledge to become evident.

SUCCESS The more you use your intellectual and spiritual capacity, the more powerful it will become. Only unused intellect fades. That you can keep a clear head under pressure will show that your knowledge and beliefs are correct for you.

FIVE OF SWORDS

This card represents the quintessence of the weapons and the tools of intellect, mind, and spirit: We can learn from our own and others' experiences. Everything is difficult before it becomes easy.

Take problems and worries seriously. Take care of desires and passions. You don't need to be afraid of these vital powers – quite the opposite! Use the power of the swords to make clear and honest decisions: Fulfill wishes that make sense and make them your motto. Recognize wishes that don't make sense and let them go. Take genuine fears seriously and prepare yourself. Discern fears that are not legitimate and let them go.

FIVE OF SWORDS

LOVE Don't throw in the towel. Don't let others put you down. Be ready for criticism and self-criticism. You will find a new approach and more understanding.

HAPPINESS "A river rises from the depths": Suddenly you understand the very different phases of your life in their contexts; you see the "central thread". Look for the *sense* in victories and defeats, and respect the value of experience that is reflected. Your happiness grows because love and insight grow.

SUCCESS New successes are needed: You grasp the sword and make yourself heard, even if your theory is not fully developed or perfect. That's ok. Because how much of the power of superiors comes from proper authority rather than from our near endless patience, our shocking powerlessness? A healthy impudence saves you from making yourself look small.

Six Of Swords

Six Of Swords

You have set off and are traveling with others. The six swords can be ballast or useful equipment – just as the people in the image support each other.

Is the ferryman setting off for new shores, or is he the restless commuter between the worlds?

Clarify your interests and needs. Let your intelligence be like the stake in the image: an aid that can support you because you have contact with the very *bottom*. Don't forget where you came from and where you are going to.

Old and new experiences mix together. "I have been growing along a wall I have smashed the stones but I still carry their pattern" (H.C. Flemming).

LOVE What applies to you doesn't apply to others – respect the distance, difference, and necessary translation to others. Understand the needs of your fellow men. And bring them to understand what motivates you. Use all your powers of combination and mediation so that it *flows* between you and your fellow men – and you can navigate your own course through the stream of events.

HAPPINESS Look for *experiences* and the motives *behind* the lessons. Understand what others *basically* mean by them, what they do or say.

SUCCESS Free yourself of repeating forces. Set sail for new shores!

Seven Of Swords

Seven Of Swords

Every person brings a new truth into the world, and each of us encounters certain riddles that are only there so that we may find the predestined solutions.

You decided for yourself and have therefore opened up the path. There is a lot of courage in this, but, above all, the intelligent insight that you can best help yourself and that doing so is also the easiest and most effective option. Emphasize every step. This card is always given cunning, intrigue, futility, and other unedifying meanings, if you don't understand yourself and/or others.

LOVE Don't let yourself be intimidated by problems and contradictions. Go your own way. Work with your dreams and clarify your objectives in love. This is also critical for the present questions.

HAPPINESS You take what you need; what you don't need you leave. You go your own way. You realize that you have had to battle a lot of trouble and many conflicts because you had too little courage for your dreams. The longer you failed to shake off the fear of your own courage, the weaker that courage became. All the important battles take place within yourself.

SUCCESS You have to survive the many conflicts and difficulties only for as long as you have little trust in your truth and mission in this life. Understand your momentary disputes as a contribution to improved understanding of your tasks and place in the world. You will experience and achieve something considerable.

EIGHT OF SWORDS

EIGHT OF SWORDS

This stands for different kinds of mental ruling: either spiritual prejudice, entanglement, and inner remote control or inner contemplation and expansion of consciousness, above and beyond appearance and what is palpable.

Understand the fullness of your intellectual and spiritual talents. Look inward and separate yourself from habitual evaluations. You possess a rounded, solid, and mature knowledge. You just have to admit it. You don't need to do anything in particular. Stop (the extra) acting. You have wisdom and clarity in you.

If you feel trapped or biased, the card says: The swords are available to you; therefore, it is possible to cut off inappropriate inhibitions and dependencies. Get up and stand for your rights and for those who cannot do so for themselves. In the positive sense, this card invites a special commitment of a deeply personal type.

LOVE Separate yourself from restraining obligations. Be consistent with yourself and others! Develop your own rules.

HAPPINESS You become aware that you possess many skills but are chained down. You are trapped within your imagination. Something isn't right about the picture that you have painted for yourself. Don't wait for external help. Decide your own freedom.

SUCCESS If thoughts and acts link and mutually connect, you will make considerable progress.

NINE OF SWORDS

NINE OF SWORDS

A complete mental horizon is changing – it darkens or it fades away, then it aggregates and opens itself up afresh! You are to master the complexity of the "swords." This means the manifold weapons and tools of intellect, mind, and spirit

Reset the basics. If you can separate an undefined, chaotic original state into yes or no, into black and white, this will be a particularly creative action! In Genesis, the biblical story of creation, just as in the myths of other cultures, the "creation" of day and night, the differentiation between light and dark, is the *first day of creation*.

LOVE It begins to dawn on you. You become awake. Clarity breaks through the darkness. Accept it! You are confronted with alertness, clarity, and light. Get used to it without pressure. Relax. Your freedom is not a burden. It's ok to be as you are. Be ready to be really there, to act from within you and to answer for what happens. That is your responsibility. You don't need to prove anything. Be your friend and love yourself.

HAPPINESS The other side: It dawns on you. You are scared. It has become dark. It can't go on like this. You must get up and out if the current situation is not to become your jail or grave. You have chased false beliefs for long enough. Development cannot be undone. In the past, you have chosen, and now and in the future, you can choose anew. Get up!

SUCCESS Take care and protect yourself from a mental short-circuit. Add one and one together! Slowly get used to new knowledge and beliefs.

TEN OF SWORDS

TEN OF SWORDS

Here you see the fruits of the mind: Unsuitable, fruitless thoughts ruin you. However, from a positive point of view, the seeds bear rich fruit, and a consciousness grows from your existence, from your personal experience, which shows the path to great happiness and deeper satisfaction.

There is a Zen proverb that says: "If you meet the Buddha on the road, kill him!" This means: Get rid of all idols, supposed authorities, and all other outward self-ideals. The real "Buddha" is always someone other than the one you think you know.

LOVE Your previous self-definition, your ego, the image that you have of yourself is the basis of your relationships, and perhaps also a particular perception of love, happiness, or success. That can be painful, shocking, or releasing. In any case, you are alive. Take the situation as it is. There are many "right" callings, loves, and successes.

HAPPINESS Take possession of your strengths and freedom. Accept yourself without particular preconceptions and prejudices. The death of fruitless dreams, ideas, and theories allows new, shining horizons to emerge. In place of firm concepts, constant controls, and justifications there emerges the power to accept the moment, to decide in the situation and to answer. Being alert to the demands of the moment brings great happiness.

SUCCESS Be ready to work without an example. Your breathing and thoughts should flow calmly. Stop overly *worrying* about everything.

PAGE OF SWORDS

PAGE OF SWORDS

This card represents free and adventurous thinking as a *brainstorming* exchange provides a multitude of ideas and associations. Intellectual movement or "tilting at windmills"? The "flag flying in the wind"? Pleasure in intellectual experiments?

Ensure a long, deep breath of fresh air. The value of a new idea is not measured by what it is but rather by what it *will be*. Protect yourself from "arguments" that are simply drawn out of the air. Be careful with your beliefs and those of others. Protect yourself from good faith and ignorance. Find out iwhich holes in your knowledge you should avoid and which not.

LOVE You can approach and convince other people with your ideas. In doing so, you are energetic, spontaneous, and open-minded. Don't give yourself unwanted commitments or dependencies; where you commit yourself, you are reliable and ready to take responsibility. You have no claim to the absolute truth. New knowledge and new concepts are your thing. Test new ideas and new approaches.

HAPPINESS You are an intellectually moving person. You contradict the leaders and authorities gently and wildly, you reveal weak points, make suggestions for improvement, and always have lots of new ideas. You go your own way and don't allow yourself to be assigned a particular role. Insist on further explanations.

SUCCESS Hold the sword in your own hand. Don't allow others to judge for you.

KNIGHT OF SWORDS

KNIGHT OF SWORDS

The *Knight of Swords* represents sharp intellect and radicalism. High-flying zeal and fantastic enthusiasm can play a part in the present questions.

As the sword stands for the air element of the intellect, to take action here means mental action. Reappraise your judgments, expand your thoughts, and summarize your knowledge. Thus you will bring light to your questions and draw clear conclusions. Go all-out in your decisions: Favor solutions that promote your integrity and satisfaction in the long term.

LOVE You are an outspoken, energetic person, with courage and the willingness to take risks. You don't want half measures; you are extreme about this. You want to learn the whole truth and try out new truths. "Because if one loves something, something that really one can barely have, something that seems inaccessibly far away, one will be a bit sad./One becomes a dreamer. Or a radical. Or a radical achiever of one's dreams" (Susanne Zühlke).

HAPPINESS Leave the thought categorizations behind you. Don't hide behind what "one" does or says. Develop your own ability to reason. Besides, radicalism does not always mean great – or even hectic – activity: Often even little movements and changes in everyday life have a large impact.

SUCCESS The goals have to be right. Then you have great power and readiness to surrender yourself and to experience and achieve a great deal.

QUEEN OF SWORDS

QUEEN OF SWORDS

The *Queen of Swords* represents two opposites: love and despotism. With her sword, she is also reminiscent of the card of Justice. As the *Queen of Swords*, she stands for mastery of the weapons of the mind. So, you are to achieve just judgments, correct thinking, and approved knowledge. The better you understand and respect the other sides, the strangers, the unknown in your life, the easier and the more untroubled you will judge and rule.

Be careful in your assessments and loving in your evaluations. Whatever happens, *there is an alternative (if not several!)*

LOVE You are a strong, regal person with great power and a pronounced sense of justice. You consistently and rigorously insist on clarity. You fight repression and dependency. You preserve your freedom and that of others.

HAPPINESS "Freedom must be boundless above the clouds" (Reinhard Mey). The boundlessness of experience causes fear. You know these fears – you overcome them by living with them. This gives you great power to involve yourself in situations and events, to always be fully present. You evaluate people according to your experiences in the situation, not through preconceptions or current idols.

SUCCESS Look behind the scenes of alleged practical constraints. Risk a free, independent opinion. You have nothing to lose but your own prejudices. Cast off obstructive responsibilities. Show what you are made of.

KING OF
SWORDS

KING OF SWORDS

Heaven and earth represent theory and practice, spirit and nature, but also free will and practical necessity.

It is the task of the swords as *weapons of the intellect* to communicate between the worlds, to carry out wise exchanges and necessary discrimination. The *King* stands for sovereignty in these things. You have and need a lot of knowledge and an active conscience, and courage to be unconventional. And you must be true to yourself. Protect yourself from enthusiastic, idealistic, or cynical mind-sets.

LOVE You are an experienced and conscious person. Your strength is your clear, far-reaching view, which you have achieved through long debates with yourself and your environment. You examine the world. You design your life according to what you consider to be right. If you want to know something, you are very rigorous and insistent, even with yourself.

HAPPINESS Great visions and passions are hiding within you. At the same time, you are especially able to organize your life yourself. This sometimes leads to difficult and painful knowledge and decision processes. But you owe it to yourself to find your own path and persevere.

SUCCESS Preserve and strengthen your personal independence! Hold on to the unlimited possibilities of the spirit and overcome the concrete necessities that lie before you.

ACE OF PENTACLES

ACE OF PENTACLES

The face of the matter. This card stands for the calm, emotional, and moving energy of the earth. The Ace of Pentacles is rounded off in the truest sense of the word – endless like a circle or matter. In matter are life and dynamics.

And: You are like a coin yourself. On the one side, is the question, "What minted me, what created me?", and on the other side, "What will I mint and create?" Like a stamped coin, every person has excellent and less excellent parts. Every person has particular strengths and particular handicaps.

The acceptance and transformation of these characteristics in total define one's personal talent. Sometimes, great events communicate understanding of this; sometimes it is more inconspicuous "hair-splitting" that provides insights into the real understanding of personal talents.

LOVE What does the earth have for you? A cushy number? Like the Titan Atlas, carrying the whole weight of the world on your shoulders? Grasp the power that hides within you and make the contribution the world is waiting for! Take hold of the world with creativity and passion!

HAPPINESS The card signifies a happy, rounded life with everything that you need on this planet.

SUCCESS "We have inherited the earth from our parents and just borrowed it from our children." Nothing is without consequence, and nothing becomes lost. What traces does your existence leave behind on earth? What enduring values are you creating?

Two Of Pentacles

Two Of Pentacles

What you consider valuable and valueless can change. You must balance them particularly well. Be wary of the "coincidences" that happen now in your life and decide whether they have something to tell you or not.

Your chances and tasks are connected with freeing yourself from assumed constraints. There is an alternative – always at least one! In the moment that you use it, you discover your own weight and your part in what is happening. You are not the servant but also not the master of the situation. Here, "all or nothing" doesn't help – nor does playing dice or quarreling with fate.

It's more about your skill, about a lucky hand with the existing challenges and chances. It is time to take leave of some attitudes and agendas that used to be very characteristic of you but have since become worthless. Other values and areas of life are entering your life. The development of your personality is already a blessing!

LOVE Expect unexpected confirmations, and with them uncertainty, if familiar realities are to be expanded into new dimensions. Don't be afraid.

HAPPINESS Every real change is connected to a reappraisal. The focal points of life change. Previous basic rules were ambiguous, striking habits appeared conflicting, and new tasks approached the old ones! You are standing *in the middle of it* and learning more about yourself *than ever before*.

SUCCESS "Invest" in your personality development. It is good for you and at the same time stimulates the most important part that you possess.

THREE OF PENTACLES

THREE OF PENTACLES

This card is about the clearing, the differentiation, and the transformation of your personal talents. How do you love and accept your particular strengths and particular handicaps?

Various aspects of work, occupation, and vocation are the topic here: the working of the material, the redesigning of the earth, the work on yourself, the release of your own character. And further, the work with and on others. Also the questions: What does this work contribute to? Who uses it? What is it based on?

LOVE Don't allow yourself to be deceived, and don't shy away from confrontations with dark or unknown affairs. You will discover hidden talents!

HAPPINESS You understand work not only as a necessary evil. For you it is also fulfillment and pleasure. You need such work. It won't always earn you a living. However, if it reflects you and is your specific contribution, then you can always earn money with it or make the available employment suit you.

SUCCESS You follow your calling and find meaningful work. Your dedication leads to another type of work. At some point, the end result or some deadline is no longer important, but rather it is the work process itself that is important. You experience that your contribution is deeply embedded in the entirety and that it is effective; that additional or secondary activities are an important part of your work.

FOUR OF PENTACLES

FOUR OF PENTACLES

"A professional in your own things": Clear out whatever doesn't suit you. Discover the world and make your place. Create new designs and suitable standards according to your personal values.

Everyone has special talents. Make sure these pay their way. The most valuable talents are those that provide the most good. They are most beneficial when as many wishes as possible can be fulfilled and as many fears as possible can be dispelled.

LOVE Love is not just about feelings. Love also means mutual support while forming your own existence. Give others the key to yourself. Emphasize the specialness of your position. Let others take part in your world.

HAPPINESS You have talents that distinguish you in your own personal way. With your knowledge and abilities, you create a satisfying possession, a solid basis. Enjoy your qualities and admit your abilities. Don't spend time with pretenders and sneaks.

SUCCESS With this card it is sometimes important to consciously set a limit in order to prove your personal intrinsic value or simply to discover and investigate it. However, sometimes it is also much more important to share, and to let as many other people as possible have a share of your abilities and skills. Consider the community. But also insist that it takes into consideration your particular talents and tasks.

Five Of Pentacles

Five Of Pentacles

"The self-assurance is sometimes only frozen and comes to life when it is thawed" (Wolfgang Ambros). Poverty, suffering, need are the subjects here. *Or* deliverance from them!

There is an old legend telling of the blind and lame walking together. The blind is supporting the lame and the lame leading the blind. By sharing their needs, they overcome their individual helplessness.

LOVE Even "weakness" has its value. Consider a different speed of development. Always compare like with like! Accept joint responsibility. Don't let yourself be pushed into unproductive dependencies or agonizing obligations.

HAPPINESS The borders have no foundation: Just like the borders that previously provided you with security or a home, they have shown themselves to be deceptive. And so the borders that separate you from peace, happiness, and the feeling of having arrived are not forever or insurmountable. Begin to accept your disruption or your search. You are entitled to be happy. Start being good to yourself. Take care of yourself. Spoil yourself and let yourself be spoiled. Make it easy for yourself and arrange your life accordingly.

SUCCESS Trust in the happiness of friendship and the blessing of cooperation. Contribute to ending unnecessary suffering. Help the world to become more human, economical, and comfortable. That does good and brings huge success.

SIX OF PENTACLES

SIX OF PENTACLES

The pentacles are well structured in this picture. So, you are to look for a good structure in your relationships, your tasks, and your results. Work with all resources and get them in good order. Realize and appreciate being part of something bigger than yourself.

LOVE Not all good things come from above but from yourself. Inner balance is important for you. You create an atmosphere of nearness and exchange, in which the differences between big and small, weak and strong, are minimized. Create a situation in which you can be weak without provoking strength (and vice versa), a situation in which you can take and receive without scruples or going down on one knee.

HAPPINESS The joy of giving: Not the charitable giving of things that you no longer need; not declared self-abandonment in the assumed service of a cause or idea; no, your own ability, your beliefs in giving your best, taking your dreams seriously and doing something concrete towards them. In this sense, you have only what you give away and don't keep for yourself.

SUCCESS The well-structured metabolism with others – this productivity is the key to your present questions. Create and retain a win–win situation. Thus you will make the world more valuable and your personal life more satisfying.

SEVEN OF PENTACLES

SEVEN OF PENTACLES

Irrespective of whether you have a lot of work before or behind you, this is about a balance of your previous results and definitions of new goals. Are you happy with the results? With what you have worked on?

Your results are a mirror of your life. They show that emotion or clarity of thought is, in the end, only worth as much as you can transform into results, and equally that your results and products only bring happiness and satisfaction if they are an expression of yourself.

LOVE Use the reflection in order to make clear what is important for you. It's only about results that are valuable for you. If you confront the results you will find love at your own level.

HAPPINESS There are certain riddles in life and practical tasks for which you find the solutions only in that moment when you also recognize *your* importance, your personal sense, your life's task. Every solved task shows you that you are on the right path. Even a *mistake* is also because it clearly shows what isn't part of your task and assignment.

SUCCESS Lovingly and critically handle the existing standards. You must search for clues and interpret signs. Every circumstance, all the facts, tell a story and have a meaning that is worth studying and interpreting. Therefore it's also about your own interest, your own point of view, and your actions!

EIGHT OF PENTACLES

EIGHT OF PENTACLES

Mastery: Every task that you overcome is also a mirror of the work on yourself. The more clearly you work out your own talents and limits, the more you will be master of your own affairs.

Your mastery lies in the *multitude* of personal talents. Ensure numerous results that carry your signature, your cut, and that you can recognize yourself in.

LOVE Attentiveness is the order of the day. Love is at times a delicate flower. Not everything works first time; rather a bit of patience is required. But that doesn't hurt.

HAPPINESS You are a connoisseur. You know that everything is important, not just the end products, but also the accompanying circumstances. You are your own boss. You go step by step. Your work has a character of letting grow, and you grow with it. That makes your actions pleasant and allows a lot of really worthwhile results. It creates a situation of personal abundance: Not every showy and extravagant luxury, but an abundance of well-being, realized ideas, and fulfilled wishes: "a lot was unnecessary and particularly that which was the most needed" (Edith Vahrenhorst). You have this art of the most necessary.

SUCCESS Relax and stay awake. Understand the message "between the lines." Be ready to learn something new. Take care not to "preach" to others.

NINE OF PENTACLES

NINE OF PENTACLES

What about the boundaries in your life: Protection or barrier? Do you trust other people? Do you trust yourself?

You are free to choose in each moment – choosing "yes," or "no," or "both." The secret of flourishing cooperation is the respect of each party involved. This is the foundation of a successful common creation.

You may give respect to others if you respect yourself. And vice versa – you may respect yourself if you pay attention to others. In this way, together you create something bigger than the mere sum of individual properties.

LOVE It is a good card for winning new friends and having new fun with old friends. You have a certain composure, you know: You always have what you need. Be brave, swallow your pride regarding pettiness and jealousy.

HAPPINESS If you *and* your fellow people approach each other with caution and love, then a fruitful, pleasant life situation will arise in which everyone has their own kingdom – and in which you find your home, with your strengths and weaknesses, your advantages and disadvantages, in short, with everything that you possess. You cannot make a bigger "win," and you should not be satisfied with anything less …!

SUCCESS The rose can only reveal its full beauty when pruned correctly: You rigorously renounce unnecessary ideals, unwanted obligations, and non-binding experiments.

Ten Of Pentacles

Ten Of Pentacles

Optimum results: Your experiences and those of others flow together to form a greater whole. You know that you can't hold onto anything, that changes cannot be avoided, and that they contain opportunities.

You understand how you build on things done by people before you and how the next generation continues them. Yes, time is just relative. You recognize yourself in both young and old. There are no limits that lead to an end, nothing vanishes if you find yourself in the past and the future and bless the present.

LOVE Love is the best benchmark, and not only for the closest couples. It is also what gives us reliable orientation in the web of daily encounters and events. Therefore, risk giving more love and a little bit less exclusiveness at the same time. Accept many people and incidences in love every day.

HAPPINESS You find your happiness in satisfying relationships and your home. Everything you need is there: spiritual and material well-being, a moving equilibrium. You have a large range of possibilities and stimulations, a new experience of putting down roots and arrival. Where you are at home, you will learn to fly. And where you learn to fly, you will create your personal field of energy and stay within it.

SUCCESS Promote the talents of as many people as possible. Understand and respect the tasks that others give you – this will bring you great success.

PAGE OF PENTACLES

PAGE OF PENTACLES

Our own talents appear unimpressive, either because we don't consider ourselves important or because we have a false impression of what is important and believe only specialists or stuntmen have a special talent. In reality, however, every person has special talents because he/she embodies particular experiences and expectations. You "just" need to find the value of these potentials, and this card is a good occasion to do it.

You have to filter the familiar and to look beyond the main stream: Your own talent is also always present; you just don't recognize it immediately. Be prepared for new practical opportunities and use them!

LOVE Don't let difficulties discourage you. Don't forget that beauty and truth often lie hidden and must be found.

HAPPINESS Your "pentacle" is a gift from life; it mirrors that you are a *treasure* for yourself and your environment if you recognize your talent.

SUCCESS Every practical improvement, every gain, and every new financial chance is also connected with it, so that you better understand your talent – your gifts and tasks. Check your experiences and results. In this way, you can pick up the coins, the gold lying in the road.

Knight Of Pentacles

KNIGHT OF PENTACLES

There is something to finish and *harvest* in this life and today is the day to do it! Now is the time to complete some tasks with deliberateness and composure. Don't shy away from necessary confrontations. Have faith in your ability to solve problems, do away with fears and fulfill wishes.

You create a pleasant life situation that is based on your practical attitude towards life and the recognition that your life is in flow. You live uninfluenced by superimposed ideas that would pull you away from your core.

LOVE The joys of the *Pentacle Knight* grow out of his understanding of natural limits and the unity of all life. "The art is knowing how to set limits," and this gives you the maturity to let go and let yourself get involved. Thus love becomes the central thread in everyday life.

HAPPINESS You are a strong, calm person. You stand in or before tilled land and can let things grow. You know you only live here and now, and for you it is imperative that you make your life pleasant and comfortable. Your strengths are quality of life, the concrete extra, and a personal "reasonable" luxury.

SUCCESS Short-cuts on the path to success: Forgive yourself and others for not being perfect. Also, the waste that we all produce is still usable – as fertilizer and humus. You can't change your fellow men, but take them according to their talent and apply them so that their talents are optimally brought to the fore.

QUEEN OF PENTACLES

QUEEN OF PENTACLES

A card of reflection of the real values. Your calling is to make a difference, to realize the value and special wealth that your existence means. Talent is a duty.

Feelings of arrogance and inferiority are only obstructive in this. Do not flirt with your chances or difficulties. You possess particular gifts and particular handicaps; the ability to make something significant of enduring value is special.

Concentrate and relax: Everything has its moment; everything takes its course, which you cannot change through interfering and agitation or indifference and waiting.

LOVE You live according to your gut feeling, deep-rooted and passionate. You are familiar with the cycles of coming and going, of birth, life, and death. It gives you a lot of warmth and an erotic charisma. Anyone you protect can move without worries. Take good care of yourself, too!

HAPPINESS If you draw this card, it is about sovereignty in the practical design of life. Differentiate between top performance and false ambition. Understand your part in the world and make an impact.

SUCCESS Paths and detours, difficulties and exercises, are part of it, if you want to achieve your personal peak. Allocate your tasks so that you can also master the mountains of everyday life: "Do first what is necessary, then what is possible, and suddenly you are doing the impossible" (proverb).

KING OF PENTACLES

KING OF PENTACLES

You are a creative personality, and a down-to-earth conscience gives you strength and endurance. "It makes no sense to demand from the Gods what you are able to perform yourself" (Epicurus).

What are you waiting for? You are a connoisseur and, at the same time, the planner and organizer and someone who finds peace in life through your work. Prove and develop yourself as the architect and master builder of your life. Finish tedious duties – or change them into work that you can enjoy.

LOVE You are calm, determined, funny, and luxurious. You need clear circumstances and a solid basis to be able to thrive in life and relationships. The way to the heart is through the stomach and all the other senses. You create an atmosphere of well-being, security and pleasure.

HAPPINESS Work and pleasure, passions and duties, old traditions and new discoveries – you can combine your different tasks and talents into one complete production – a work of art – a life's work. That means strong efforts, but also many gifts received, as you are letting things grow.

SUCCESS The card of planning and managing assets: You are your own capital – fields and harvest, vineyard and wine. Create a balance sheet of which important goals you have achieved and which are still missing. Create supplies and use reserves.